MW00982207

The Choreography of Desire
Poems and Photographs
by Diana Hayes

THE CHOREOGRAPHY OF DESIRE

Diana Hayes

Rainbow Publishers
Vancouver, B.C.

Canadian Cataloguing in Publication Data
Hayes, Diana, 1955-
  The choreography of desire

  Poems.
  ISBN 1-55056-638-5

  I. Title.
PS8565.A88C46 1999   C811'.54   C99-910024-6
PR9199.3.H3678C46 1999

Published by Rainbow Publishers
#29 - 4900 Cartier St.
Vancouver B.C.
V6M 4H2
dehayes@islandnet.com

Design & Typesetting:
George Payerle Ltd.
Uri Cogan & Tim Collins

Cover Design: Pat Walker, Illustrator
Cover Photograph: from "On The Way To Mektoub", Diana Hayes
Author Photo: Bill Almond

Printed by Friesens, Altona, Manitoba, Canada

Acknowledgments

"The Wishing Cross At Gleann Dá Loch" appeared as a limited edition broadside, Christmas 1996, dedicated to my parents John & Frances, Beannacht ar an mhuintir síorraí, printed at Lightning Press, Salt Spring Island. The broadside has since found its way to the Gleann Dá Loch archives with many thanks to Sister Dolorosa, Dublin, Ireland.

"The Body of Grief" and "When A Stranger's Skin Tastes Like An Alder Fire" were written for the "First Annual Salt Spring Erotic Literary Evening", March 4, 1995.

"Fallen Angels" and "Running Hwy.101 West" are both dedicated to Sheri-D Wilson and were conceived during a freak snow-storm in September '95 while we were on retreat in Alberta at the Bucking Fillies Ranch.

"If I Were There With You Tonight" is for Tim, aboard *Klytia*.

"On The Way To Mektoub" appeared at *The Body* exhibit, Exposure Gallery, Vancouver, September '96. My narrative for this sequence owes a debt to Geraldine Brooks who describes so intimately the "hidden world of Islamic women" in her book *Nine Parts of Desire*, and to Wade Davis in his book *Shadows In the Sun – Essays on the Spirit of Place* from which I quote his definition of mektoub.

"Of Bodies Changed to Other Forms I Tell" was exhibited at *Full Frame III* at the Hong Kong Bank Atrium, Vancouver, November 1996.

"Delphinium's Transubstantial Dream" was featured at the *Unseen Light II* exhibit, Exposure Gallery, Vancouver, April 1996.

Photographs from all three sequences were included in *A Gathering Of Images I & II*, Salt Spring Island, December 1996 and July 1997.

Many thanks to my photographic mentors, Betty Peters and Bill Almond, who have both shared their enthusiasm, expertise and darkrooms.

For embodying the dreamscapes and helping to bring these visions to film, I thank Roben Doobenen, Michael Doward, and my dear friends Diane Baxter, Art Falardeau and Haidée Virgo.

Thanks also to Brian Brett, Patrick Lane, and George Payerle for invaluable editorial assistance.

I am grateful to the Canada Council for providing me with a short-term arts grant which enabled me to complete this manuscript.

Thank you also to Tim and Russ, who both danced with the muse.

CONTENTS

PART III

Pegasus,
who taught me first to run, then to fly

"The eroticism of visual representation consists, precisely, in the illusion that the flesh is permanent."
Carlos Fuentes

Nothing of natural substance is permanent. What we are seeking through erotic expression is to defy the cycles in nature. Death, "the great stepmother of Eros", turns a blind eye. We are dying every minute of our lives yet under the veil of Eros we glimpse the infinite. There we can believe the body is timeless and thereby will transcend the laws of the natural world.

Everywhere the landscape is shifting and changing, ebbing and flowing. The impermanence of nature is nowhere more apparent than at the seashore. Creatures rise up and reveal their frailty and their strength as each wave washes our eyes. Yet it is this suggestion of the infinite that arouses our vitality and brings us to the lap of Eros wishing to sing.

PART I

WHEN A STRANGER'S SKIN TASTES LIKE AN ALDER FIRE

When a stranger's skin tastes like an alder fire,
    When he tastes like dusk, mid-July, orca's oil seeping the inlet, bodies
languishing on yachts as the halyards keep rhythm for a sheltering sun

When a stranger sails his schooner snug into the harbour,
    walks you down the night beach, tide up beyond the rocks, slipping,
helps you find your footing with his hand, fine whiskey in a glass, no shoes

When a stranger tears the shoulders from your dress clean,
    kisses the pit of your arm while the fire flames alder in the sand, dances
both hands in slow circles past your knees, kisses again the pit of your arm, wet
with mid-July heat and smoke

When a stranger calls you Undine, calls you fey, tells you Paracelsus knows no
alchemy for this, pours sea water in your hair, mercury rises and licks the sand
from your face

When a stranger speaks a tropical language, intonation of consonants,
measured breath in tongues, speaks words from a forbidden book, chants
the chorus from his throat, words rising and falling like an oboe on the wind,
nearly decipherable

Cuando la piel del forastero sabe a fuego del eliso

Forastero, mío, cuando te deslizas entre el crepúsculo
y la noche,
tu piel como estrellas de alabastro que se muevan
bajo la mirada de la luna llena,
como seda entrepierna, bebiendo el elexir salado,
bebiendo el hambre de mis hojos

Mi, forastero, intrépida sirena de tantas canciones, la cera
de Ulises se ha caido de mis oidos
I ahí encuentro tu lengua,
El calor, ancho como el arco de la playa, el calor quemando
el mastil, quemando el hambre de mis hojos,
el calor de tu sexo

    that's what he says

When a stranger takes you into his net and bends you until you think you will
break, bends you clear of the moon, swallows you whole, drinks your sighs,
bends you more

Breaks your heart when he leaves your harbour, leaving the taste of an alder fire
on your tongue, in your hair, everywhere the taste of smoky skin, your legs
dripping the night,

When a stranger's skin tastes like an alder fire, all the next day

Cuando la piel del forastero sabe a fuego del eliso

THE BODY OF GRIEF

The body of grief has no shame
The body of grief tears back the sheets and lays his weight on your chest
The body of grief knows no limits, takes a bite out of your heart, is all fingers
                                                        and teeth
The body of grief always tells the truth, won't let you sleep for weeks
takes your breath away, speaks from the gut in low persistent groans,
The body of grief wears a five o'clock shadow, makes your chin raw with his
                                                        kissing
The body of grief walks in your boots, licks your toes,
The body of grief gets into your jeans, won't leave you alone, follows you home,
takes up the whole bed, sleeps with his head on your thigh, fucks you in
                                                        your dreams
The body of grief rocks you on the dance floor, pours another drink, puts his
tongue in your ear, sweats in your eye, stings
The body of grief has no shame, licks your tears
drinks your eyes, leads you to water
makes you crazy with life again

IF I WERE THERE WITH YOU TONIGHT

I would reenact the stars, set a candle's glow
across your naked cheek and reach the centre
of your breath with my bare, clear heart.

If I were there with you my love
the night would not begin to end
but stretch its limbs to reach our torque and element
as only night and the burning sea could recognize.

Your eyes unfold the long journey
from fields and wells unknowable
where we had fled and fallen and fled again, not knowing
if our breath would last another incandescent night.

But here in arms, the full stretch of body's length
I call to you, I say give me your mouth by night
give me the tongue that sets my lips afire
muscles taut in tandem glow, the days when nights
were few and only small imagined beats
of bodies raised this illumined song
until I knew my sight might fail but oh, the tactile
notion of your thighs became me, devoured my call
until the breath, in unison, calmed our wounds
and covered our eyes in tranquillity.

ON THE WAY TO MEKTOUB

ON THE WAY TO MEKTOUB

The Tuareg, a nomadic tribe of the Algerian Sahara, named from the Arabic "The Abandoned of God", hold to the tradition that it is the men and not the women who should veil their faces after puberty. Although the Tuareg are Muslim, their interpretation of the faith allows women much sexual freedom prior to marriage and encourages close platonic friendships with men after they wed.

The writings of Paul Bowles, particularly his stories "The Delicate Prey" and "A Distant Episode", and most of all his novel The Sheltering Sky *have obsessed me for years. The arid expanse of the Sahara has entered my dream world with all the ritual magic of a Bowles encounter, in shades of baked clay and ochre. One dream in particular had me perform a rite of passage in the bay of a nameless Moroccan town where the medina reached down to the sea, and while witnessing my crossing, a tribe of veiled men and women urged me through the red and menacing water with their chanting – the slow falling away of the hijab.*

With these preoccupations in mind, I set out to describe the body in images that would obscure the usual definition of feminine and masculine principles and, with the slow winding and unraveling of the veils, illuminate both the ambiguity and the interplay of the male and female forms. How we cover and uncover the body in various rituals and traditions, how the expressions of the body, disguised or veiled, mirror the inner landscape, and how the body moves and dances in the particular environment, were all ideas I wished to explore in these images.

The use of infrared film assisted in locating the feminine in both my subjects, with the Agfapan film providing the contrasts and the texture to capture their masculine energy. At times the boundaries blurred and both subjects were transformed by the particular light.

I placed them on a north-west facing beach in the Gulf Islands, yet somehow the variety of textures in the midden mounds provided the austerity and mood of the desert. The sea was a welcome oasis.

I named the sequence "On the way to mektoub", after a quote I found on the making of the Bertolucci film:

"There is a silver thread that reaches from the base of the spine to the heavens, where it becomes interwoven in the fabric of destiny. One's own will is meaningless. All is written. This is Mektoub, or fate.... In the void created by the absence of will, the spirits of light and darkness have room to move."

PART II

RUNNING HWY.101 WEST

I can go anywhere with these legs
all the messages feeding my nerves with go, go forward,
go up, go beyond yourself, your hunger is your compadre
your hunger makes you move in the eye of the muse
your legs cross the double-line highway of your heart:
you are bare, raw, uncluttered, able to see directly into the sunset
looking west beyond the Rockies, that is where the weather turns, that is where
the deep green shadow of the forest rises up and clips the edges
of your wings, making them more aerodynamic,
moving down the prairie highway on two good legs
they take you there, don't need new fuel, remind you to breathe
give deep relaxed beats—song, sigh, song
sigh and expel the rage, there is no room for cramped breath, begin a highway roll
past greener fields, past fenced houses, past trucks on a road with no shoulder
to lean on, keep going, this is better than love it lasts
and will not leave you hungry
without breath, will leave you full again
sweet sweat beading down the passages of your body
everywhere no matter what the temptation the water is slick
and you keep running to the beat, to the beat, to the beat keep running

FALLEN ANGELS

At sixteen, on the ski-hills of Banff, our bodies
were alive with snow. Nothing ever ended.
Our hunger the size of our world,
our limbs became longer in the shade
skin white, perfect porcelain with every curve
          and lean turn
our Celtic blood had not unfolded the many
layers of darkness, how when we learned desire
we also learned the suspended music of our hearts.

Let us say we were descending the mountain
clear of prevarications, sightings
no map could discover as our bodies
grew hard and wet, fingers playing madrigals
          across our ribs

Let us say we were exquisite dancers
with all the savage epiphany of this chinook
with all the intention of summer
all appetite for our lovers
as they made melting angels in the fallen snow.

LOVE NOTE TO THE CYTOLOGIST

Skin of skin, bone, milk . . .

Deliver me from your restless stare
put back the bites you have chewed, the needle tears
the eye of fear not blinking the weeks ahead
find a gem of light
a fragment gift of salt
what I am made of, not torn but one

just give me your tick
of approval, the sting is nothing
compared to your wayward heart
don't let your colleagues convince you
a planet doesn't talk and the earth is flat
paint my slides with rouge, give them lips
embrace the glass casing
with all the rogue and incubus cells
of my daemon, my daemon, my daemon breast
get up and dance across the lens,
across the delusions of the clock
and all the dark and risky filaments
that stalked me in my years

deliver me from your latex touch
see a star in flesh, a perfect orbit
go on to bigger things
why not take in thighs, or other caverns of lust
I'll spin you on your petrie dish
give a twist to your
all too grave reflections

Skin of skin, bone, milk . . .

Don't after all these nights
take my flesh, my desire away.

WHEN LOVE GOES HUNGRY

The shy couple go looking for a vessel for their love. Between kisses, they try on boats. Elaborate yachts with double masts, bright spinnakers, elbow room. But their love gets lost in teak and they choose a simple rowboat with oars of fine pine and set out to find an island for their love.

The winds are north by north-east and the rowing is a challenge. They take turns with the oars but each discovers their best side and as a consequence the boat turns in circles, never making any headway, never getting far enough from shore to believe they are really going somewhere. So the woman takes the left oar and the man the right, and together they blend. The boat begins to disappear off the edge of the horizon and they know then they are really on the journey.

During the voyage, they recite haiku, wanting spare language, wanting only the best words. After three days they notice water is low and food failing, not imagining they require anything to survive. They make love in the late afternoons when the sun burns an amber quilt of light at the edge of the sea, and the golden hue softens their hunger and their orientation. They drift in the dream of bodies, skin sliding like twin fish spawning the ford, all else slipping just the other side of the horizon. The music of their memory sings still notes and they are pleased they have so much to bring, so much within the simple boundaries of the boat, their bodies, their love.

A fortnight passes, and they see as their destination a great round disc of land, with foliage and stone, with trees bearing fruit. This is Alpha, the circle of desire, the island that will contain their love in every direction. They have joined the sea-birds and the fishes in a celebration of this cycle. A tower of stone becomes their castle, with moat and fishes and growing heather. The tower stones caress their hands, telling them they have finally found a vessel for their love, inviting them inside to lay their bodies between hearths of fire, hearths of wind, hearths of time.

In the night, they squeeze their bodies between makeshift walls and rest within the perimeter of their creation. Here they dream of snowfall, great gales of surf, a wind that would put a candle out behind a pane of glass, the strong hollow notes of a wooden flute calling their hearts, offering them another way. They are discomfited by the dream they share and go to opposite ends of the beach without words. There they meditate upon their desire and find the wind subsides, and the images of snow become images of feathers, and lightly the quills brush against their cheeks and breastbones and give them peace again. When they walk back across the beach they do not recognize one another and their bodies begin the dance of newness, circling skin, circling hair, circling lips, over and over they untie their bodies in fire.

Then begins the rationing of food. Then begins the leave-taking of the dream. Then begin the first, unfamiliar groans of hunger that cannot be comforted by the kiss. They go out at night. They look for ripened fruit.

They collect baskets of food, combining their luck at the end of the day. Fish refuse to come close enough to shore to be caught. Shorebirds perceive the inner workings of a famine and will not interfere. Shellfish hide and birds will no longer roost in the bare trees. Slowly one by one the small creatures return to the sea and are silent. All else goes dark and they hide in their skin, sleeping night and day to rid their minds of this shadow. All vision becomes mute. All songs imperceptible.

The woman, in her confusion of hunger and loss, goes out. She finds a tree where several bulbs of fruit are waiting. She returns every day to watch their growth and succulence increase. They speak to her in effortless voices, charming her with their scent. They touch the skin on her face and bring back the life there. They dance around her legs and kiss her ankles. They are all-encompassing. Her mouth never stops watering in their presence. She goes back every day at the same hour and waits. She imagines their firmness of flesh between her lips. She imagines the sweet pulp in her throat. She imagines the blood that will flow in her body when she reaches up to touch. She imagines each day, at the same hour, and under the tree where she rests her back against the trunk and moves in slow circles until the heat grows.

On the fifth day following the full moon she is woozy with temptation and reaches up to break the fruit from the branch. Her eyes are blinded for moments in the eclipse of her mind and body and when she opens them the fruit is gone. It is simply gone. Did she see it? Was it there? Her mouth is dry and she is no longer hungry.

She returns to him mute and exhausted. He is keeping watch on shore for fish and does not notice her wasting body crawl back into the tower. Within the walls she dreams again.

In the dream she is a tireless crone, tending the fire. She is in the arms of her own death, comforted. She does not need food or shelter. She is still and listens to her voices.

When the man completes his watch she sees that he is gone a long while into the sparse foliage of their wasting island. When he returns he is distracted and full of torment.

She observes him and her silent voices say there is something gone missing from him. There is something seeping from his skin that leaves him bare and cold. She reaches towards him but he is silent. She searches his eyes but they are stone. She imagines his hunger is more profound than hers and offers him the last pieces of fruit from her basket. He shares this taste with her in a kiss but after that their mouths never meet again. Her ribs begin to show. Her belly is hollow. Soon a vague illness overcomes her and the veils of confusion sink around her ears. She is lost. There is nothing else to do but wait.

After three years she is unrecognizable. She no longer has hair or colour. She is content to sit looking out to sea, waiting for the oar-maker. Waiting for the row-boat to take her home again.

The man constructs a signal light of glass and tries to capture the eyes of passing ships. He is invisible and no one can see him now.

She watches how he goes down the beach every morning as he has always done, and contemplates. She watches him from the corner of her eye and is puzzled by his strong body, the moisture of his skin, the sure steps of his feet. She looks at her own body and it is all bones. Her cheeks are hollow and her eyes are without light. He returns from the end of the beach and tells her he knows nothing that can save them.

Each night by the fire he repeats her story of the fruit when it came down the branch to kiss her. He asks again and again if she kissed the fruit. She is haunted by the shadow of her memory. Did she bite or did she kiss the yellow globe? Or did she only imagine? She thinks and rests and thinks again.

On their final night, the air goes very still and the darkness is thicker than the sea. They sit, as they always did, on opposite edges of the beach looking out. And then the floods begin, and the winds and nothing is left inland but the torn branches of a restless tree. They find their way into the oarless shell of their boat and with the last branches of this dying tree row and row until they find land again.

Two moons pass and the woman discovers the dried stones of fruit in the man's coat. His pockets overflow with the traces of greed. He has already fled for the ridge and cannot explain the presence of this food, cannot explain the flesh still on his ribs, the colour in his cheeks and the kisses on his lips. He cannot explain that by his hoarding he has set her free.

OF BODIES CHANGED TO OTHER FORMS I TELL

OF BODIES CHANGED TO OTHER FORMS I TELL

I had not yet read Jane Urquhart's Away *when I woke from a dream in which I was summoned to the body of a near-drowned fisherman off the shore at Santorini. Suddenly I am transposed to the island of Rathlin watching Mary — Moira — breathing life back into her sailor. Yet my dream was distinctly set on a bay in the Aegean; aquamarine, with fine white sand and black-haired villagers frenzied on shore surrounding the washed-up body of a nearly departed young man. I was called from my reverie to his side as it was clearly my task to persuade him back to this world.*

All objects and characters in our dreams represent an aspect of our psyche which requires expression and ultimate resolution. When I set out to photograph my semiconscious sailor I did not understand that by way of giving back life/breath to the dream, I would myself need to surrender to the image.

The west coast landscape creates a universal canvas for dream imagery, and although the reference points in my dreamscape were distinctly Greek, I was able to recreate the emotional texture on the Southey Point beach. Seeing my semiconscious sailor dashed upon the rocks was startling to me in the same way that my dream confronted the near-drowned nature of my own life at that particular time. The often androgynous quality of dream characters is fitting for such a sequence, particularly as all characters ultimately merge with the dreamer.

I was often in the water during the shoot and once again came to understand the strange seduction of the sea – how we are all drawn to our own fate in ways we cannot tell. The tide was 10.5 that evening and required thigh-height wading to get to the little bay of my choice. This means of arriving by way of a journey reminded me, as always, that it is the process, the narrative, that holds up a mirror to our secret longings and frees us from the constraints of our daily lives.

The title for this sequence comes from Ovid's Metamorphoses *which Jane Urquhart so aptly quotes in the early pages of* Away. *I think it also apt that my Aegean Pacific sailor should come to life with the help of Ovid's verse.*

PART III

THE WISHING CROSS AT GLEANN DÁ LOCH
ST. KEVIN'S BIRD AT DUSK

What transforms the fields beyond Laragh's green road
while near light dazzles the eyes of mares
as they bolt, then prance to the rough fenceline?
What desire there, under the moss
to soothe the tangled vines of the footpath,
leading my steps one beat forward; not untidy
or hesitant, the body reaches another day,
                    another continent of time.

Feral sheep with luminous coats flag the way in a chorus
of instant banter, no matter that I am led by other purpose
and see their eyes glimmer in twilit memory, reaching the
breath of St. Kevin's song, each alike in their holy cell;
make-shift pasture recalls an ancient journey
                all conspire to worship.

I am only forage for the tribe,
can reach a strand of stray wool between branches
and guess that I am coveting the only longing
in St. Kevin's hands, how he reached to feel the very wool
or outline of feathers while the sparrow sang,
and cloven hooves astray in his back fields
swayed to a finer message only the fair-haired saint
                could comprehend.

Upon the Wishing Cross he would bare his desire, his
recompense heavy with self-confinement, but not in this
small world did he gather the vision of beasts,
for while aloft in remote banks of the great Lough
patterns became creations, ripples on the glass water
              grew like chasms in his heart,

so that he knew with better sense to live
confined with beast, and this alone
would drive him closer to his god
while people of the granite spine of Wicklow pressed on.
Years of squabble and feast could only heighten his solitude
for in his cell he reached beyond the greed and battlements
of the Tower, his own footing hewn in simple steps
circular to the landing
no roof or shelter to take his attention but upward
reaching, breathless, toward the sparrow's
              arcing flight.

THE SILVER MISTRESS OF OUR DREAMS

At Laragh by the Derrybawn hearth, Yeats's Glendalough singing in distant throats
I prepare for the green road at dusk, Temple-na-Skellig by the moon
not a trace on the grounds but the wraith of famine and bloody monastic soil
all else stilled in the shade of coniferous arms, the oaklands a welcome stand
since leaving the west a fortnight ago, the Poulnabrone Dolmen
                                        still reticent in the Burren.

I walk out in night's air, all holly and hazel and crisp inhalations,
thus the shaggy flock start by my rustling presence,
having felt a figure pass before in the mid-evening clarity.

Walking the rhythm of a more tenuous dance
all else falls away from the bold core, feels fretful astride this shadow
as travellers shed from vacant faces the tears of a sleeping child
while The Troubles press more deeply to their spine.
The two lakes appear in the growing perspective,
a more perfect mirror to the sky could not be found, trees awash in the canvas
all manner of songbirds nesting in the close corners of the upper lake's perimeter,
the tower lifting to the heavens like an eager phallus but torn by the dark history
of his maiden's country, reaching, singing, leaving all ordinary seasons
to herald this stone precipice, here in the glen for the world
                                        sometimes to see.

Laying down these stones, plying a life for an impossible task
safety or prowess, what matter that they built an emblem of the road tower,
even Jung's Bollingen an instrument for the larger voice.
Everywhere the sap of time spilling, the cold clutches of the nineties
running like harpies on the path before me
where this vision of abundance turns and sleeps.
Here, beyond the last chapel monuments, some collapsed
by the weight of visitors' eyes, busloads of blind tourists
are filming all they see lest their memories fail.

Near-light has fallen to the lee of the glen, on the southern bank
a leaning tree misshapen with age and wind's restlessness
waits the moon's final repose while I embrace her under the veil of the knoll.
The journey never complete without St. Kevin's bride, the sparrow
deep in the *Valley of the Two Lakes,* the silver mistress of our dreams,
the wild, *the terrible beauty born.*

So she ascends the final stairs with a look of departure growing in her limbs
then disappears amongst the oak with barely a trace,
                                        only the indescribable caress of wings.
I look out from the fair Saint's cell that once conveyed this homage to nature,
the last requiem to his god's good earth, and curse the blood that makes us man
and therefore blind in our homily, unable to answer the beckoning of this past
our mouths empty for words or psalms, into the cumulus wonder of days
to the Saint's resting ground, this place where the green road leads
and no human treads at such a holy hour as this, Ireland's pale and wistful dusk.

THESE HANDS

These hands have travelled the morning mist in autumn
to find the last, the final golden leaf torn from limb,
catching the updraught to land upon a new world,
her purpose and moisture now gone, transferring knowledge of trees
in a smooth caress, as I place her on my round table.

These hands have tasted the many winters, looking for embers
long chains of ritual, the gentle curve of another
leading to the nest
and in small gestures, they tell me not to despair
that hibernation will bring fonder dreams
and the luxury of deep stillness
while the mind is coaxed and buffeted through the short days
given sentiment and endless time to wander.

These hands have jostled the manes of half-trained horses
and plaited the ritual into their dance,
speaking down the length of leather to the sensitive urging
of a mare's mouth, who in her tentative submission still glows
with the herd, still rises above the turf in her element of
complex beauty, to become partners with my desire.
These hands take her gently beyond the rhythm gait
to find the subtle partnership of two animals crossing
the wide trail to the night.

These hands go astray in a foreign tongue, urge me to look
beyond the camouflage of smiles to the mirror in the wound
have a chorus of moods too easily transformed by song
and the bold vistas to the south.
They can only know truth as a weanling trusts the source of milk,
mouths knowing the shape and avenue of an only world.
These hands have nourished a tired crew while keeping watch
when all is trodden and misery the size of stars.

These hands follow me to sleep and become tendrils
for my journey, leading the way to unknown edges,
trusting all that governs the tides while mending the wounds
in transit, these hands can bring the radiant warmth upon the shore
as with certain sea creatures in spring.

ON THE ROOF, THE PAINTER BEHOLDS HER MUSE

Painters on the roof creep between vines
of fabric with their eyes, seeing the sleeping lady
in dream's perpetual time.
What picture in their minds glows past the bewildered
hunger of their stare?
In what perfect centre have they placed
their clumsy hands?
The sleeper dreams, does not waken
cannot interpret their diaphanous wings,

for the dream becomes the muse
and curled upon her side she strokes his seldom skin
for just the way in which he moves so gracefully
from mouth to breath to lips,

how he is all aflesh with laughter, can make
a double-fire with sticks from the mating dance
beholds without the uncertain chemistry of words

is effortless in her sleep, where over again
he turns to find her face
just one last brush of skin while stirring, she sees
the ghost of the painter's eye, seeing not one but two
alight the lace veils of upper story world

and all she can do is smile at her intruder
colouring the fabric of her muse
with words only silkworms care to spin.

DANCING THE NEW MOON, NEW YEAR'S EVE

Unravelling time, this spool of thread, letting the days
wash their backs in a wintering frost, cabin lit
with smoke fires, fast fire moving between arms, the notion
of risk hanging in the eaves of a long December night.

The scent of this man talks to me, tells me
I have been a prisoner in my skin, learning again
the unveiling search to dance. Eyes like mercury move
too quickly for focus, and mouths eat the ripe mango
orange flesh drips our chins, plays in our teeth
like violin strings sounding in the candle glow.
Bite the skin I say, taste the spice
inverting discs of flesh, sucking the year from juice,
sucking the spice surprise, sucking the life-force
like this, our winter's desire.

We walk into the star-drenched sky and in braille
find our way to the forest path. Passing gates and a
slippery bridge, chickens hear us whisper past the coop
and greet our steps with inaudible clucks, bearing down into
the nest for New Year's eggs.

I have a small light at our feet.
I want to take your hand but don't.
Every tree becomes a leaning post and every fern a kiss
against our backs. I lift my coat,
I show my heat, I dance your hand there
while voles and mink watch, feigning sleep
and the phantom cougar breathes toward his rival,
animals with little fur, foreign tongues,
aching to taste the scent on your fingers, the scent on your
mouth, all the words and gestures that have passed here before.

To the sea we continue, necks reaching back to take in
the full arena of stars – and Venus, laughing at our hunger
reminds me to breathe through my feet, winter rings of
Saturn and Jupiter in the mind's eye.

I put my hand in your pocket and the world of flesh
ignites the path, I breathe the scent at your neck
and in one bite of air the sea changes colour, unfolds a
silver glow, moving tides that ripple to our feet.
We are at the edge of the rockface, unable to step
forward or back, just up and down
our bodies like fish, like spawn, the animals we are.

DELPHINIUM'S TRANSUBSTANTIAL DREAM

DELPHINIUM'S TRANSUBSTANTIAL DREAM

The subject of human transformation, both psychic and physical has preoccupied my work for some time. In the realm of our dream lives, we may mingle with archetypal figures and through deeper investigation can be transformed by these encounters. Learning the particular language of our dream world can provide a lifetime's journey and source of creative strength.

In Delphinium's Transubstantial Dream, I set out to capture the essence of a dream that seemed to presage my life at that particular junction. Delphinium was the homeopathic remedy that induced the dream during which I was entirely changed from flesh to vapour and then to dust. My consciousness had no boundaries. I could feel the collective energy of all that existed around me. I experienced a profound sense of completion and peace that has no parallel in my earthbound state.

The photographic sequence narrates the five stages of this process: sleep moving through impatience, acceptance of light moving through transubstantiation, and finally the achievement of grace.

Photography has always felt like magic to me and working with infrared film is truly an alchemical process. The heat-sensitive film quite literally captures "unseen light" and the results are often unpredictable. During the shoot my subject was immersed in the narrative of my dream and became immune to earthly elements, particularly the cold of early February. It was the early hours of the morning and a hint of sun appeared just in time to illuminate the textures of our setting. At times it was difficult to distinguish the photographer from the subject. Somehow, in the creative process, we both became the dream.

NOTES ON AUTHOR

Diana Hayes was born in Toronto in 1955 and has lived on both coasts of Canada. She studied at the University of British Columbia and University of Victoria, receiving a B.A. and an M.F.A. in Creative Writing. She was Poetry Editor for *Prism International* while at U.B.C. from 1980-82. Her poetry, articles and fiction have appeared in various journals including *CVII, Descant, Event, From An Island, Island, The Malahat Review, Poetry Canada Review*, and her poetry has been broadcast on the CBC. Her published books include **Two of Swords** (co-editor), **Moving Inland**, and **The Classical Torso in 1980**. Her play **Islomania: Saga of the Settlers** (an historical collage of early pioneers on Salt Spring) was produced by Salt of the Earth Productions and for the Salt Spring Festival of the Arts. She has also researched pioneer life and characters in the Tofino area for adaptation in poetry and short stories.

Recently, Diana Hayes has expanded her poetic vision into the realm of photographic dream and narrative sequences. Her photographs have been shown through the Vancouver Association of Photographic Arts and the Exposure Gallery in Vancouver. Her photo-sequence entitled "Delphinium's Transubstantial Dream" was chosen as promotion images for the *Unseen Light II* show in April '96, and her dream sequence entitled "Of Bodies Changed To Other Forms I Tell" was featured at the Hong Kong Bank Atrium for the Vancouver Photo Festival group exhibit November '96.

Since 1981, she has made her home on Salt Spring Island where she divides her time between writing, photography and monochrome print-making, theatre and literary production, and when possible, travel.

This first edition consists of five hundred copies signed and numbered 1 through 500 on 80 lb. Bravo Dull text with Rainbow 2 endsheets and Kallima C1S cover stock. The text type is Adobe Garamond 14 pt. and the titles are Footlight MT Light 14 pt. All photographs were shot with a Pentax MG camera using Kodak High Speed Infrared or Agfa APX400 film. Original photographs are 11" X 14" and are printed on Afga Brovira-Speed BS 319 PE 2 paper or Agfa Multicontrast Premium MCP 312 RC paper. This book was printed in Canada by Friesen Printing Limited for Rainbow Publishers, January 1999.

No. 68